Eternity Calling

Christian Poetry

David LaChapelle

21 Then I saw "a new heaven and a new earth,"[a] for the first heaven and the first earth had passed away, and there was no longer any sea. **2** I saw the Holy City, the new Jerusalem, coming down out of heaven from God, prepared as a bride beautifully dressed for her husband. **3** And I heard a loud voice from the throne saying, "Look! God's dwelling place is now among the people, and he will dwell with them. They will be his people, and God himself will be with them and be their God. **4** 'He will wipe every tear from their eyes. There will be no more death'[b] or mourning or crying or pain, for the old order of things has passed away."

Revelation 21:1-4 (New International Version)

POEMS

8 But do not forget this one thing, dear friends: With the Lord a day is like a thousand years, and a thousand years are like a day. **9** The Lord is not slow in keeping his promise, as some understand slowness. Instead he is patient with you, not wanting anyone to perish, but everyone to come to repentance.

10 But the day of the Lord will come like a thief. The heavens will disappear with a roar; the elements will be destroyed by fire, and the earth and everything done in it will be laid bare.[a]

11 Since everything will be destroyed in this way, what kind of people ought you to be? You ought to live holy and godly lives **12** as you look forward to the day of God and speed its coming.[b] That day will bring about the destruction of the heavens by fire, and the elements will melt in the heat. **13** But in keeping with his promise we are looking forward to a new heaven and a new earth, where righteousness dwells.

2nd Peter 3:8-13 (NIV)

Begin

No help in sight

Only faith in you

Hold tight

The one hope

To help me cope

That your way is better

Just realized

Where the pain ends

Freedom is found

To begin

Gain

Eternity is calling

I am falling

Into your arms

Your loving grace

Is all mine

When I pray

It is here to stay

You show the way

To give up the fight

Surrender what is not right

To end the pain

And gain all the day

<u>Seasoning</u>

This world is losing its attractiveness

Ambition for satisfaction

And nothing less

It has lost its flavor

We are the salt

To savor

Waiting for you

Everyday

The rest of my time

So, sublime

<u>Same</u>

Help me Lord

Waiting expectantly

For you

To show me

There is nothing more to do

Embrace your grace

In your loving ways

Ending the struggle

To look over my shoulders

Freedom begins

It is all the same

<u>Him</u>

Give up

The fight

To retain

What is right

I take flight

Into the night

Ever so slight

I will be alright

It is His might

That is tight

Set Table

The promise of a better day

Is only a moment away

A game you cannot play

It is an illusion

Fused with delusion

Only one winner

A table with dinner

With the Lord

Forevermore

<u>All His</u>

Bless me Lord

Show me

What is all for

To come to you

To open the door

To be my rescue

From guilt and strain

No more pain

Give up control

Let go

Take my soul

I am all yours

Better

Your ways are higher,

than my ways

Your thoughts are higher,

than my thoughts

Cannot chart my own course

Show me the love

To give up the fight

To fix the wrong

All around

Your tune sings a song

A hopeful melody,

of something better

Wake Up

Give up your rights

Give up the fight

An illusory ideal

Was stealing my zeal

Letting go of control

Freedom found

Around the corner

In my soul

My joy

Forevermore

Belief

I surrender

To your heart

Tender forever

Not plotting my hurt

I feel that now

It was all me

Fighting for survival

I need a revival

Everything I ever need

Help me to continue

To believe

First

I trust your timing

To start climbing

Answered prayer

Come forth

Life's manifestation

Hope

The last will be the first

It is going to hurt

For those who do not believe

You will see

The destiny fulfilled

In these last days

Staying

Looking ahead

Messes with my head

Celebrate the small

Victories in life

Make the bad fall

That troubles my soul

Is the way to live

Progress

Is found

In knowing Him

Where I am now

Is just the beginning

Surrender

It is not my battle

It is not my war

I am not keeping score no more

I surrender all my needs

To your glorious grace

Less of me

More of you

Your favor

Never wavers

Some displeased

Rising above

The scene

Turn

Evil people are everywhere

Or should I say

the lost who stick together

like glue

No clue

Repent and see

His majesty

Working in strange ways

He loves you

Do not let the enemy

Fool you

Turn

Love

Wicked brought down low

There in a corner

Wearing a frown

There is now way to discover

They can still be found

No more room

To maneuver

Decisions left undone

Do not make a mistake

And be left out

Call on Him now

The lies are no more

Go through the open door

He will be waiting for you

Love

Rest

The sun is going down

Shadows fading fast

The light is calling

Your name is not going to last

Do not be ashamed

See the truth

For what it is

Take a better look

Do not be taken back

What you had is gone

He will love you

In His arms

Replacing what was lost

And so much more

Trust Him for your salvation

That is revelation

Act Now

The lost are in a corner

There is no place to boarder

The end of decision

Has arrived

Derision does not have to be alive

Two paths to take

One that leads to life

The other forsakes

Should not even mention

It is not a new invention

Come to the convention

Supper is waiting

Do not be hesitating

<u>Forgive</u>

The time has arrived

For punishment to thrive

To force the hands

Of those who do not understand

To get them to see

God is love

And wants them to choose Jesus

He will forgive you

Whatever you did wrong

You can have a new

Play a new song

For release

Make you whole and complete

Right Side

Come to the cross

The kingdom awaits

To live in peace

The rest of your days

A love that cannot be described

Do not run and hide

Do not discount what,

you do not know

He will show you

An open door

Take a chance

And be on the right side

Needs

I am so in love with you

Knowing I do not,

have to save myself

You take me back,

And will bring me,

to your loving grace

Showing me how to live

A life in stride and in place

I know you

And what you are about

Take me as I am

Cannot do without

Guided

Trying to save my life

Like I know better

Then who carries me

From beginning to ending

What is good and right

I cannot discern

Just guided by the Holy one

Giving up control

To who restores my soul

Whatever you have planned

Humble me Lord

Before your throne

<u>Seeing</u>

I believed the enemies lies

For the last time

A double minded man

Full of tears

Cannot explain

Did not know,

which way was up,

which way was down

Spinning all around

God's grace touched my life

Do not have to fight

I was full of pride

Battling God

To have my way

Not aware I am living

already free

Dependent on God

For the fruit in me

Humbled

I see Him

For the first time

A new beginning

Long Game

I am hurting

Hanging by a thread

All my goodwill for this life

Has come to an end

Lost my life for Christ

Is the only way

It was not working anyway

Brought me this far

I can say

I play the long game

It is not lame

The Bible is my guide

To show His plan

There is more to life

Then what can be seen

The Lord is coming through the sky

This I know

Why?

Because the Bible tells me so

His Way

Fear of death

Fear of losing control

It does not matter

I went to school

It is all an illusion

That torments my soul

Coming to the end

Where freedom begins

Wrapped up in,

the, Father's love

His loving care

Less of me is the eternal plan

Get out of the way

Jesus is my rescue

For another day

No Worries

Too much to bear

To cope with on my own

I need the Lord to overthrow

Full of His blessings from the throne

Want to raid the storehouse

Be patient my son

I am coming soon

Just want my way

More often than not

Have to unwind

To His loving care

Everything is there already

The best thing to do

Is to have no worries

Fool

Jesus knows the plan

To save me from myself

Come to the end

Of what I thought I was about

Step out of the way

Take a good gaze

I am in the long game

I am not lame

No thank you

Look around

The world is coming down

Who is the fool?

A fool for Christ

I will leave it at that

Locked

If judgment begins with us

What will be with the rest

of the bunch

I am glad I got know Jesus

When I could

Now everything is on speed dial,

and it hurts

It is too late to develop

Into Christlikeness so soon

Gathering us home

The beacon shining

Calling us to where we belong

He will show us more

Next to His throne

He knows the score

World Reality

Things are heating up
Faster pace takes it on
Frequency pulses closer together
The intensity is greater
Earthquakes and Hurricanes
Have not seen for centuries
Are popping up everywhere
There is no room to maneuver
Cannot look over your shoulders
To discover what is undercover
No time too
Days fly by ever so quickly
Seasons change ever so swiftly
Everything is out is open
Deception and lies take the front cover

Anything to distract you

From the true nature of things

The sky will open

The Lord will return with His rewards

And shut the door behind

For those who

Don't believe

In His name

Showing

How, long Lord,

Do I have to wait,

For your loving Grace,

To light the way?

I cannot stand it anymore

Show me an open door

So, I can be free

Who I am meant to be

I doubt you Jesus

What is this all for

Have to give up

What I am holding onto

Is less of me more expensive

Help me believe your intentions

Your will is better

Than any convention

With God

Turn me into a Saint

So, I can paint

This town

With Jesus' love

More from above

To open the eyes

Of the blind

Heal the land

See a better plan

It is in your hands

Show me what I can

Do with you

More than I can do

2nd Chance

Depression is condemnation
Thinking you are not enough
Short of God's glory
The fall

Shame says you are bad
Not knowing what I do
Is not who I am
Freedom is around the corner
Come unglued

Guilt is I have done wrong
Even if nothing is going on
Now I am aware
The Lord can heal

The pain of the past

That seems so real

Surfacing in the present

To be released please

God breaks the chains of slavery

It is over my shoulders

Forgiving me

It is all Him

Hooray!

Forever

Everything is out in the open

There is no room to hide

Truth revealed before our eyes

Bide your time

For the ride

He will be by your side

Showing you the way

To a better day

Where you can stay

In His loving arms

Forever

Hooray!

Game

Long term man

You have a plan

That stands

The tests of time

No other fines

To pay to get good

Shed blood on the cross

Did it all

Forgiveness

Forevermore

You have settled the score

There is no more

That we have to do

Just believe in you

And trust you to come through

For there feelings of due

There is nothing to subdue

Me

What are you going to do?

For a man who is unglued

Can you piece him back together

Or will you make something better

To weather

The storms in life

Growing to the next level

More strife

More strength

More favor

Open my eyes

To see the love in disguise

That you are sovereign

My Lord I am the problem

That gets in the way

Solve the riddle

Of my heart

Put the puzzle together

A picture forever

That will last all eternity

You are making me to be me

Love Me

When will this end

This game that is so vain

It is lame to believe

You make me like this again

Born into sin

Who's, fault is it anyway?

Just trust in you

To make me like new

After all I have been through

What can I say

It is not my scene to play

Just overcome with you

You loved me before

I was in my mother's womb

Easier

Burn off my ropes

Furnace to cope

Impurities in scope

Protecting the pain

Creates more strain

Defences brought down

Releasing a frown

Dismantling me

Is a full-time job

Like eating corn on the cob

God is the salt and butter

To make what is difficult easier

ABOUT THE AUTHOR

David LaChapelle is a born-again Christian since the year 2000. David has earned himself two Computer Technical Diplomas from Seneca College in Toronto, Canada in 1994 and 1996. He graduated with a Psychology degree in 2011 from Trent University in Peterborough, Canada where he now calls home. David lives a quiet life and enjoys writing and being an author. He is proud of his works and hopes it will bring him recognition in this life and rewards hereafter. David is a firm believer in reading the Word of God and the power of prayer and wishes the best for all humanity awaiting the Lord's return.

OTHER BOOKS BY DAVID LACHAPELLE

David's Adventure with Schizophrenia: My Road to Recovery

David's Journey with Schizophrenia: Insight into Recovery

David's Victory Thru Schizophrenia: Healing Awareness

David's Poems: A Poetry Collection

1000 Canadian Expressions and Meanings: EH!

David's Faith Poems: Christian Poetry

Freedom in Jesus

Canadian Slang Sayings and Meanings: Eh!

The Biggest Collection of Canadian Slang: Eh!

Healing Hidden Emotions for Believers

Breaking Clouds: Christian Poetry

Walking Light: Christian Poetry

David's Faith Poems II: Christian Poetry

All books and e-books available at Amazon

Manufactured by Amazon.ca
Bolton, ON

38976930R00031